AF732577

A GOOD BOOK

VICKIE T. WARNER

Copyright © 2022 by Vickie T. Warner

ISBN Softcover 978-1-956998-57-3

All rights reserved. No part of this book may be reproduced or transmitted in any form or by any means, electronic or mechanical, including photocopying, recording, or by any information storage and retrieval system without express written permission from the author, except in the case of brief quotations embodied in critical reviews and certain other non-commercial uses permitted by copyright law.

Martin and Bowman
1-855-921-1348

CONTENTS

Introduction 1

Dedication 7

The Preparation 9

The Process 13

The Purpose 29

The Praise 39

Conclusion 53

Prophectic Postscript 59

About the Author 63

INTRODUCTION

A book destined as a bestseller is hard to put down after it has been affixed to an inquiring mind. This manuscript is colorful and appealing to the eye, coupled with a catchy title stirring the creative mind with a piercing introduction, quickening the adrenaline of the reader. It is specifically designed to ignite the reviewer to launch into every pulsating detail revealed from the explosive synopsis, ensuring excitement, and great anticipation regarding the enriching contents in this book.

In the twinkling of an eye, perusing this book has effectively steered the curiosity of the individual to this interesting narrative compelling the reading of this book. No doubt, the innate probing of humanity triggers the search for the unknown to enhance or empower them in their search for the mysterious.

As a result, the author's sentiment and purpose to sway readers has been accomplished, because the individual's curiosity has been awakened by this vivid, and interesting heading, in anxious anticipation readying them to interpret the inside contents. All of this, due to the inspiring of a mental quench stirred by the colorful cover. Thus, encouraging the viewers to dive inside: to discover the essence and magnificent ingredients instilled in this exceptional book.

Now, picture yourself as the book and bestseller. In fact, "you are" the manuscript engaging, the mind of man with your stunning spirit: life adventures, literary lessons, trials, tests, and testimonies; rousing the excitement of curious seekers, anxiously seeking to read the enriching contents of your life. Moreover, as they turn the pages of your yesterday, the new chapter of each tomorrow reveals the divine gift of God's grace that intrinsically led you to the magnetic light of Christ. Because of this, the viewers open the glorious ingredients of a regenerated life serving Jesus, to motivate them to enhance their biographies to be and build a terrific book.

The bible records a story of king David, being identified as "the man" who committed sinful acts. David's life was an open book depicting tales that shaped him into becoming a man after God's own heart. David is likened to us. After all, he is depicted as a man, who had failures and faults, acknowledged by him, because he was born with a depraved nature. He recognized this and attributed this disposition to being born a sinner, (Psalm 51:5 NIV). We are all familiar with the cardinal sins that David committed, adultery and murder that required some serious whiteout from God.

Because of this, God sent Nathan the prophet to David, and he told him a parable (that is a story) about a man whose life God had prospered and yet, he coveted his neighbor's wife. After hearing this, David was furious with this act committed by this man, and decreed, "this man must die and pay for these horrendous acts." Nathan blatantly informed him, that he was "the man," (2 Sam. 12:7 NIV). David had just pronounced punishment for this man, after hearing about his sinful deeds. He demanded justice and his command was to be obeyed, even though David did not know, that he "was the sinful man" in this story.

David was "the man" that selfishly desired what his neighbor had, and through abusive authority, manipulated another's man wife, impregnating her, and then commanded the murder of this man to cover his sin up. What is prolific and profound in this story about the command of David is that the mercy of God meted out this unjust authority. The Spirit of God convicted the heart of David, moving him to repent for the sins he committed, and accept the divine discipline that would impact his household. His repentance was the whiteout of God, which is revealed in the life of David, whose life has been an open book masterfully written and inspired by God.

Repentance changed his life. Many people struggle with this misunderstood word. That simply means a change of mind initiated from a heart acknowledging sin and decides that correction is advantageous for their wellbeing.

King David's life was depicted to stir you mentally to consider this man whose sin story will forever be told, in how he was shaped into "a man after God's own heart," due to the merciful whiteout of God. David was chosen by God just like He chose you. "The Lord sought him a man after his own heart, and the Lord hath commanded him to be captain over his people, (1 Sam 13: 14); "I have found David the son of Jesse, a man after mine own heart, which shall fulfill my will," (Acts13:22). Thus, liken unto David, your life is the open book you live, that is presently being read by others while God is working providentially penning tales about you as His chosen vessel. God desires to get the glory for this manuscript as the Author and Finisher of the faith in His creative works, manifesting another chapter and bestseller with your name existing in the Book of Life, (Rev 35:5 KJV).

Surely, the prophetic words of Moses' prayer ring true "that we live our lives as a tale untold" asking God to: "teach us to number our days, that we may gain a heart unto wisdom," (Psalm 90: 9, 12 NIV). When in fact, his plea is that faith produces lessons in our life experiences to apply wisdom and make every day count as counsel in our relationships. Pondering this, Morgan Freeman has a stunning voice that calls hearers to attention when narrating storylines. It has an alluring tone that captures and keeps your attention as you anxiously await the conclusion. This voice analogy resonated with me relative to listening for guidance through the story narrative. Hearing is paramount in guiding the viewer through the narrative from the beginning to the end revealing the explosive contents. Just as, Morgan's voice masterfully guides you through the storyline, the voice of God is the holy guide in the life of those walking by faith. Your life journey depicts the living narration of God's voice in the good, bad, and the ugly in how He ordered your steps to make you a "good book." The story unfolds in the development of environmental disciplines, crisis and worldly challenges. This is what I call the preface, of your book. God destined these trouble trails to draw you and your critics to Christ by successively working through these tasks to nurture the transitive spiritual renewal of humanity to perfect the image of God.

Christ in us personifies the Creator of humanity, who ascribes you like a good book to imitate God the Omniscient Master and Overseer of all events in our life. Whereas His penmanship records the factional rudiments of worldly writings to describe one's faith, and finality from His point of view, disclosing the events influencing their conversion and new life in the spirit. Picturing this, the Author pens descriptive details based on our lives as tales being told revealing His divine process predestined for us; to awaken God's purpose for His chosen people. Therefore, personifying the man, molded by this Potter into becoming a bestselling book; honoring the Author and Finisher of His faith, because he is deemed a divine manuscript revealing the grace of God.

As you read this manuscript, I am depicting myself as the "good book" highlighting my humanity and spiritual lessons I have gained in my life, due to the conditions of the climate and conflicts that attributed to me deeming myself a novel. It is my prayer, that you will be moved by the Holy Spirit, to examine yourselves and ascertain your life story, to determine if you are in proof text, ready for print or copyright ready and deemed a bestseller.

"For it is God who works in you to will and to act according to His good purpose."

—Philippians 2:13 (CSB)

DEDICATION

First, giving honor to God, who is the head of my life. He is the One who Rules and Reigns as the Shepherd in it. He is my heavenly Father. In addition, I reverence my husband, Rev. Avery G. Warner, my partner in matrimony and fellow minister of the gospel. I acknowledge my deceased father, Leroy Atkins, and my dear mother, Hattie Mae Murphy. Honor is esteemed to our amazing and awesome sons: Christopher, Avery, Brandon and Deontay. My magnificent and marvelous daughters, Zenitha, and Jessica. Fabulous and favorite grandchildren, Deja, Marien, Christopher II, Christian, Aubrey, Dallas, and Mallory. Accolades to my supportive darlings Byrd and Ariel. My family and friends, whose names are too many to call, because it would equate to tributes forming another book. Truly all of them are worthy of honorable mention, for their contributions to my life story. My sisters are recognized: Shandra, for her kindred spirit, support, and sacrifices in my servant endeavors, Lethia, for her fervency in pressing through the chapters of challenges by the grace of God cultivating a new foundation, and my sister Tonya, whom God has used as the apparatus to produce greater in others, who are yet to discern the virtues in them formulated by the hand of God. I salute these ladies because they are appropriated and appointed contributors to my life story used by God penning me as this book. The Mitchell legacy is honored for God favored me to be a descendant from this family. Notable members are our deceased matriarchs O'Leavy and Brooksie. Departed siblings Verbera, Mary, O'Levy, Wilma, Clarence, John T, and Melvin. Favored surviving queens, Pauline, Hattie, Juanita and Venita. A special group of individuals must be recognized affectionately deemed "the dream team." Zenitha, Chris, Jessica, Shandra, Pop and Eric. They have been instrumental and must be commended for their contributions and devotion in bringing the visions for REST and FLAME to pass. To my Christian mentors and advisors who have encouraged me and imparted wise counsel, I am grateful for your obedience to God. Lastly, it is not my intent to omit anyone, so please know, that all of you, who have supported me, prayed for me stood with me, and loved me, I am truly blessed because of you. I know, God is pleased with you and for that, your reward of faithfulness is providentially being prepared to be released in your life!

THE PREPARATION

Whenever an exciting script is deemed epic it is greatly publicized commanding prestige to the author for this great book. It is usually followed by the echoes of the readers and written reviews of the critics. The endorsements of persons who read it, encouraging others to purchase and peruse this great script, to determine for themselves if the attraction is authentic and worthy all of the hype. On the other hand, if a bestselling novel, paperback, or hardback manuscript can draw this kind of national attention; imagine "me" as a scripted literature and my life an open tale.

Imagine me as the gallantly flowing attention-grabber, gracefully adorned with natural beauty, and a divinely crafted countenance specified as my royal covering magnifying me as a bestseller. This is because, I am fashioned in the image of God and blessed as His fearfully and wonderfully made creation, (Psalm 139:14 NIV) a human creature, He called "very good," (Gen. 1:31 NIV). Not only that, but imagine me as the book rousing this kind of interest due to the admiration of my character. A reputable book that intrinsically shines by displaying elegance and a magnanimous magnifying honor and humility that prompts a propelling grasp of the viewers' attention and gracious esteem for me. No doubt, a book like this must be shaped by the divine hands of God.

Society's interest can be prompted by negative behavior and the corrupt disposition regarding your well-being and that of others, rousing the attention of critics to question your "good." Again, I am reminded of Moses' words, "we spend our years as a tale that is told," (Psalm 90:9 KJV). Moses makes this profound statement in prayer while interceding for the Israelites, twenty and older, who were sentenced to death by God because of their apostasy, they were deemed faith deserters. They doubted His sovereign authority that freed them from Egypt bondage and His promise of a permissible path to their new home deemed the promise land. Moses interceded on behalf of his suffering brothers and sisters, witnessing the death of their loved ones, knowing that God's judgment was sure, praying that they would learn that faith writes the longevity of our life narratives in the great edition called the Book of Life. Providential presence is now uttering these same words to us, through the voice of the Holy Spirit raising hope and awareness perpetually to motivate this wisdom to future faith generations. He encourage people to treasure the years lived on earth, because our divine Novelist view it as an open storybook disclosing a superior relationship with Him.

This Novelist connection is paramount for us as kingdom citizens, my preferred identity, specifying our relationship with God, since religiosity conforms Christianity to culture dictates. For this reason, distinction is paramount, identifying God as the *Author and Finisher* of faith novels. The One that orchestrates each one of our biographies as the Creator who began the chronicles of our lives *before* we were born. "Before I formed you in the womb, I knew you, before you were born,

I set you apart; I appointed you as a prophet to the nations," (Jeremiah 1:5 NIV).

The supreme Novelist set me apart to begin proofing the paragraphs in my epic narrative and has been perpetually making corrections, and changes to my story due to human frailties causing the grammatical and punctuation errors in my life. In addition, He inserted marginal additions and crossed out mistakes in my story. The proficiency of God's plan for your life is phenomenal, and only revealed when you begin to seek the fullness of who He is. This is the only way you gain knowledge regarding your spiritual heritage. For me, this was disclosed learning that there are phases in our lives in which God employs to develop us. Dr. J. Robert Clinton, in his book, *The Making of a Leader,* describes different processes of leadership growth, pertinent to us maturing as adults. One specific process is Sovereign Foundation. In this phase, God providentially works through family, environments, and historical events. This begins at birth. You might find it hard to believe, especially since the contributors were not all godly influences. Yet, God was, and He used them, to mold you," (Clinton, 1988, p. 37). Until now, I never really understood how the good and the bad experiences in my life, were being orchestrated by God in the process of me becoming a good book, successively through the impact of my development and experiences from a baby, adolescent, and adult maturation. God ordered and ordained this positioning for me providentially for my progressive perfection one day in eternal glory with God. Thus, these things are recalled in the chapter of this book, known as the process.

"One of life's greatest tragedies is that the majority of the world's population is composed of individuals who have negotiated an agreement with mediocrity, signed a contract with the average, and pledged allegiance to the ordinary."

—Miles Monroe

THE PROCESS

No doubt, my Author has been busy positioning me by delicately reviewing structural deficiencies due to numerous mistakes in how I conveyed and conducted myself. For instance, I grew up a quiet young girl, the oldest of three sisters and of course, we all had our unique personalities. I always had an ear, for as my mother would say, "grown folks" conversations, while some would say "I was just nosey." I was always listening to them talking; because what they talked about was remarkably interesting, especially some of the subjects being discussed. Such as: family gossip, feuds with friends, neighborhood issues, work, bills, and heartaches many of them were experiencing. It was at these times; I often heard a lot of pain in their conversations. One day, while at my grandmother's house, she was angrily scolding my mother and aunts. She was expressing her fury with how they were allowing themselves, and their children to live in homes where they were being habitually abused verbally and physically. As a result of this, they always ran to her house on Fridays for a weekend getaway. Only, to spend this break, supplementing their problems with alcohol, partying at the club and then returning home to the same situations. My grandmother was angry with them because she was using *shockingly strong* profanity. I believe she had a curse word for every alphabet. Although her expressions were emotionally charged, I could hear the pain in every word spoken to her daughters. I was unaware that I was learning an important lesson about how to discern verbal heartache.

After the smoke settled on Saturdays at my grandma's house, on Sunday morning she would take all the grandchildren to church. My grandmother was a faithful usher at Flipper Temple A.M.E. Church. Her worship attire was always her white uniform, white handkerchief, and white shoes; richly glowing and ready to serve the Lord. However, as soon as we returned to her house after service, she changed her clothes, we ate a good dinner and then she put everybody out! I thought, I just witnessed her singing and praising God, and feeling good with a huge smile leaving the building, only to get home and tell her daughters, and grandchildren, "it is time for ya'll to go home." I wondered why she would send us back home to the same abuse she fussed at my mother about. I was learning how in life the inflections and functions come together for a purpose. As I stated, I was always somewhere listening when adults were talking. I remember, one occasion, I was at my grandmother's house, and she was up early chatting. I did not know who she was having this conversation with. Whoever it was, she was speaking in a loud voice to this person. I proceeded snooping and to my surprise, there was no one else in the room but her. She had a piercing cry in every word, that made my heart sink. However, what really moved me, is what she was saying. Her monologue involved the same concerns she expressed to my mother and aunts about the abuse in their homes and how it was affecting them, as well as their children. She was lamenting how they were mentally and emotionally blind to it and drowning their troubles in alcohol while the kids were behaving badly. While listening to her plea, I heard so much pain in it as the tears poured from her heart. Later, I realized why she made sure she took us to church and why we had to attend Sunday school. She was sowing faith seeds in our lives, that would begin growing and be the fruit that would sustain her grandchildren. Considering this, I later learned her dialogue was called "prayer." My grandma Brooksie was pleading to God on her children and grandchildren's behalf to deliver us from trouble and to lead us to Him.

Being reared in an abusive environment contributed to me being a silent sufferer, shy and sheltered. For this reason, this eventually led to immature mistakes and deliberate acts of disobedience. Despite my attitude at times, I was never disrespectful to adults. I attribute this to the seed that was sown in my heart when I read and heard God say, "honor your mother and your father, "(Ex. 20:12 NIV, Ep 6:2 NIV). This command is decreed in the Old and New Testaments because it is a perpetual command for the longevity of life generationally. Although, I do recall a time when I dishonored my mother, unknowingly and unintentionally, due to the manipulation of an adult. This was a person that I trusted, that encouraged me in immoral behavior.

As a result, I learned the hardest lesson of my life from this about trust. In fact, this painful lesson revealed to me, that you can be corrupted by the influence of individuals you honor, who can and will mislead and encourage you in immoral habits and relationships. This is due to what I deem a pain predator. A person whose instinct for pleasure is obscured in suffering to survive. The person you know, may be a pain predator and permitted instrument used by the Author as the antagonist. After all being a good book, would make you the protagonist in the novel. The Writer does use the issues and problems in your life to keep the reader's attention. Surely, the growing pains I experienced and what I discovered required marginal corrections by the Author; to clarify the meaning of each lesson learned to enlarge and magnify the heart contents within this book.

Moreover, the cross-outs of mercy and forgiveness became the essential component for observers to interpret this feature, qualifying the making and shaping molding me into a good book. Over the years, growing in the grace of God, in the distance of my heart, I frequently heard my grandmother's prayers. Nevertheless, I made the same mistakes my mother made and found myself in an abusive relationship, after saying to myself growing up, "I would never be in," but I had to eat my words. As a result, this is what led to the deleting of some people and pain out of my life. I decided to leave this relationship for my wellbeing and the future of my children. At the same time, I knew I did not have the strength to do it on my own. Therefore, after being invited to a revival at my neighbor's church, it was at that time I realized who I needed to help me overcome this dilemma. I had to commit to the only One who could provide everything I needed to accomplish this task, Jesus Christ. The faith to step out in the uncertainty of my life now resuscitated my remembrance hearing grandma Brooksie's faith prayers to Jesus trusting the Shepherd for all her needs. However, even after making this decision, I was afraid and procrastinated in stepping out by faith fully trusting God to be with me moving my family forward. Thus, God allowed the fire to push us out. An unintentional fire was started by my son, and the conduit God allowed for my deliverance. I had no choice but to step out on the faith I heard about and live it! Thus, this word was actuated in my life, "faith cometh by hearing and hearing by the Word of God," (Rom 10:17 NIV). I now had to trust in what I heard and learned about the Shepherd of grandma Brooksie's faith. Moving back home with my children was not easy, after being on your own. Nevertheless, I was graceful that we had a place to go, yet the abuser was still with us. But not for long, he was promptly evicted. Eventually, I was able to support my family, enrolled in a technical college and we moved into our own apartment not far from my mother. Things seems to be going well.

These events were the necessary confessions and cross-outs instigating the submissive prerequisites for Jesus Christ, my Lord and Savior to enter my heart to begin transforming me. This event taught me the distinction of how personal experiences help create inflections generating seemly peculiar functions; to propel us forward in understanding their meaning to perfect change in us. Because of them, the world is watching, taking heed making critiques and judgments regarding the contents of your life to ascertain whether you should indeed be acknowledged and proclaimed a good book. Furthermore, your cultural citizenship carnal or divine, relationships, and religion are measuring devices developing your reputation of excellence. These are daily markers making a voluminous statement as the observers strive to understand the plot of your biography while the Author is faithfully working on a glorious and explosive close.

For this reason, seeking to interpret the relationships of individuals has been the spectator's motive in judging moral deficiencies and the apparatus to prove behavior differences due to our association. One key element always weighed is the environment of a person to determine whether family influences have been instrumental in our ethical growth as adults. Considering this view, society often evaluates the emotional and mental influences in our lives because they have the most impact on us from adolescence to adulthood. Sharing my story of growing up in an abusive house supports the fact that our cultural development weighs structurally in our growth. Especially, since I later became a victim of the same kind of abuse in my home. It is perturbing at times, facing the reality of your upbringing, while at the same time, seeking to understand the acceptance of moral wrongs, that seriously impact our lives. The truth about how our domiciles and neighborhoods have influenced the hurt and bitterness in many individuals, is literally unbearable for some people.

Contemplating this, our daddy while in an intoxicated state and when our childish nuisances aggravated him, or inadequate school grades fueled his anger, would call me and my siblings *dummies,* (Shandra was not born at this time). In retrospect, we were being labeled by the words of our daddy as "stupid." Not only that, I recall being called "blackie" by the neighborhood kids. Now, this certainly offended me. Our next-door neighbor's dog name was "blackie!" Moreover, family disputes and relational conflicts instigated a thunderstorm of cruel terms that hit and hurt just hearing persons insulted by them.

That is why the childhood phrase, "sticks and stones may break my bones, but words will never hurt," was the mental and emotional rejection tag recited when we were demeaned or hit by hurtful words as the remedy to console ourselves. I know some of you have been called names worse than, "blackie." Monikers so profaning and demeaning you were frequently called that you thought your name had been changed! What was devastating about these incidents was the person or people our Author used as the antagonist inflicting this pain in our lives were the ones close to us that mere whiteout was not enough. This fix required a new page and a new chapter.

Truth be told, we were offended by the name- calling but the deepest wound came from what daddy called us, "dummies." Dummy is defined as a stupid person, or one being controlled by someone else. For some reason, the names I was called did not confine me, but they did hurt! There was something in me, that would not accept this label. However, being called "dummy" did impact our household because this insult came from the one, we adored with all our heart, daddy!

During these times, we were going to grandma Brooksie"s house, for our usual weekend escapes, and the Sundays, we attended Church School, a psalm we had to learn and recite resonated with me about the Lord being the Shepherd of sheep. I remember that they were considered "dumb" animals because they were helpless without a shepherd. This typological bond toward the sheep biblically symbolizes faithful family relationships. Often when I was enduring persecution anguish and my soul was being abused and my spirit crushed, I would hear a voice saying that "sick people do stupid things and are helpless when they lose sight of the Shepherd." In Sunday School, we were taught that there was always conflict with restless sheep that always affected their behavior. Sheep that went astray could not survive without a loving shepherd that cared enough to search for them, being the source that provided everything restless and lost sheep needed. What always resonated with me about the shepherd and sheep relationships is that the shepherd always deemed each sheep valuable regardless of their conduct.

Grandma Brooksie is the reason I learned about the Shepherd and understood why she needed to call on Him daily. Grandma Brooksie was a connoisseur in name-calling and her children inherited this from her because it was common language among them. Corrupt verbal and abusive behavior became compatible in many of my family members because this was customary in the Mitchell family environment. My mom, aunties, and uncles were called heifers, and expletives that confused me at times because it kept coming from the lady who was always praying about this behavior! Nevertheless, I knew the Shepherd valued grandma Brooksie. I know because, nosey Vickie was listening, when she prayed, she confessed that her heartache, caused her to express this anguish through the pain of profanity. Then she would break-out into a "thank you Jesus," for your forgiveness, your mercy, and grace, because despite my mistakes you always come to see about me and my family!" God was working in my nosiness perfecting my heart for people.

Name- calling is not the only hurtful thing done that contributes to our spiritual liberty and growth, but the abusive acts committed against us, be it: sexual, verbal, emotional, spiritual, and physical. The Author allowed these incidents to occur in our lives as purpose points of views to navigate His plot as the reason for our survival and esteemed Creditor for each chapter conversion. Grandma Brooksie, always called on the Lord our Shepherd because of the dumb behavior that was afflicting her, the people in our family and community. I must say, her prayers were being heard, the Bible records, that God hears a sincere and sorrowful heart, "the way to please you is to be truly sorry deep in our heart. This is the kind of sacrifice you won't refuse," (Psalm 51:7 CEV). The reason I know this, is that while I was being called "blackie" my aunt Lily was calling me "a beautiful black girl." Aunt Lily was a soft-spoken woman and it was no secret that she was experiencing emotional abuse from grandma Brooksie's cheating brother, who was openly flaunting his affair with another woman. She was always pleasant, but I discerned her pain. What is praiseworthy about this, is despite what she was going through, she encouraged me! That was supplication in action providentially working to sustain her and to save me!

These experiences motivated my desire to seek the Shepherd more, to walk me through the path of the twenty-third Psalm leading me in the path of righteousness for His name's sake (Psalm 23:2 NIV), because I did not want to inflict this kind of harm on my children nor family in words or deeds. The manuscript of my life because of these encounters was God scripted and predesignated to ensure the production of a great novel. That is, *me.* These factors are undeniable and must be understood as the pages and chapters in your life are turned, so, that you will understand that these things are necessary contributors to your book being valued in life as the good book being written.

I am grateful for the foundation of relational values, I learned through the years. Our family values were instilled in moral ethics to prepare us to be honorable and respectable adults. We were always encouraged to "be somebody," even though we did not know who the "somebody" was. Truth be told, our loved ones, did not know how to express adoration and could not articulate this to their children. In essence, they were encouraging us to be better than them and be that "somebody" that their struggles impeded them from becoming. Many of my relatives did not have a secondary education so the fundamental principles they nourished were built on righteous standards and the foundation of faith.

Furthermore, religious standards are essential to teaching and training us as children, especially since we were always in church. The principles of good were expressed by respect, honor, and obedience.

These values were drilled in me. If you were anything other than this, you were considered a bad child and discipline was sure to come. I recall, going to the neighborhood store one day with my sister Mae, to purchase some things for our mother. On the way, we discussed how we would get us a bag of chips or candy since mama did not give us any extra money to buy them. After our conversation, we convinced each other, that stealing a bag of potatoes chips was ok because we were only going to do it, one time! I gathered the items for mom, my sister and I put the stolen stuff in a place, not easily detected, and we proceeded to the cash register to check out. Immediately, upon exiting the store, the manager, who by the way knew us, came out after us and said, "Both of you girls, stop, right now!" Then he asked us, "What did we have?" we said, "nothing." We hid the chips in a place, we thought he did not know, and definitely could not touch! Again, he asked, "what do you have?" Once more we said "nothing." The manager then proceeded to call our mother. We knew then that we were in trouble!

He saw where we put the potatoes chips, but he could not touch us there, but our mother could. Are you wondering where we hid the chips? Keep speculating I am not telling! We were scolded by the store manager, cussed out by our mom, and whipped by her and our dad. In addition, she called everyone in the family to tell them what we did. Not to mention, she even told the neighbors! "Them heifers been stealing." We were fussed at by everyone who knew that we stole a bag of chips! My sister and I thought, all of this for some Frito Lays potatoes chips. Absolutely, "yes." Because of the family values we were taught and rooted in our religious rudiments of right and wrong. As a result of this, we learned a lesson regarding the consequences of stealing and firmly reminded that, it is against the law, but more importantly, it was disrespectful and dishonorable to God's command. In hindsight, this was nothing compared to the consequences meted out now by the law for stealing something as simple as a bag of chips. Now, it will cost you time in jail.

For this reason, my Author had to make some grammatical changes and additions representing growth and changes to sufficiently function in me. Notwithstanding, editorial notes of mercy; blotting out childish mistakes. Nevertheless, your life is the window for all to view, and spectators are reading and seeking to formulate their own analysis of you based on your life. In other words, how you are living.

Because of this, society or should I say, the reader is ready to dive into every pulsating detail of dysfunction in your family. As you know, stories and programs with drama are popular and command greater viewers. Scenes in the novel of your life, get some folks adrenalin going and before you know it, they have become talebearers and gossipers, anxious in their quest to read and relay all the juicy details about your life. Not to mention instigating book clubs, fellowships gathering disguised to get the tea and family feud juice, Facebook chats, zoom room gossip, and cocktail groups to discuss their perceptions and recommendations about your life! Social critics gather to critique your life struggles as book review discussions regarding the chapter contents in your book as if they are experts on societal, relational, and family matters! Truth is, we are existing in an opinionated sphere that popularizes drama rather than holistic relationships that are faith and spirit filled to encourage the greater good in the populace.

Viewers in their quest to understand the dismal and detrimental effects, that caused the errors demonstrated in one's behavior, are often reading a familiar story that reflects their life too. For me, the Journalist has purposely endeavored over the years to depict an exceptional and transformational masterpiece, making me biographically good to the reader with glory props to the Writer. Errors are ordained by the Biographer purposely for the world to see in our lives that grace is necessary for text proofing perfection. The Writer, "blots out" the handwriting of traditions dictating attitudes that have conflicted us, through the crucifixion eraser of Jesus, blotting the principalities and corrupt influences through blood distinction qualifying every book emerging in Christ a good book and renown for success. "Christ openly conquers our imperfection," (Col 3: 14-15 KJV). Essentially, this describes the purpose of the Creator of our life story, revealing how the mistakes in our lives would be removed, before "white out," was created by man.

The first draft mistake of worldly influence was removed and pardoned by God. Scripture is a written witness of the editing plan in each of us as epistles, as our individual lives are being read. Apostle Paul affirmed this when he penned, "You are our epistle written in our hearts, known and read of all men. You are manifestly, declared to be the epistle of Christ, ministered by us, written not with ink but the Spirit of the living God; not in tables of stone, but in fleshy tables of the heart," (2 Cor 3:2-3 KJV).

This is specific to character reflection of the Writer's intent in expressing faith as the undeniable invisible ink and written epistle of the transformed life because of Christ. In essence the daily news for the world to read.

By the same token, as I contemplate the perception of good and evil, the Holy Spirit recalled this scripture:

"So I say, live by the Spirit, and you will not gratify the desires of the sinful nature. For the sinful nature desires what is contrary to the Spirit, and the Spirit what is contrary to the sinful nature. They are in conflict with each other, so that you do not do what you want. But if you are led by the Spirit, you are not under the law. The acts of the sinful nature are obvious: sexual immorality, impurity (unclean) and debauchery (sin, wickedness, dishonesty), idolatry (worshipping anything but God) and witchcraft; hatred, discord, jealousy, fits of rage, selfish ambition, dissentions, fractions and envy; drunkenness, orgies, and the like. I warn you, as I did before, that those who live like this will not inherit the kingdom of God. But the fruit of the Spirit is love, joy, peace, patience, kindness, goodness, faithfulness, gentleness and self-control. Against such things there is no law. Those who belong to Christ Jesus have crucified the sinful nature with its passions and desires. Since we live by the Spirit, let us keep in step with the Spirit. Let us not become conceited, provoking and envying each other." (Galatians 5: 16-26)

There is a religious connation associated with good and evil paramount for the Editor's description and discourse pinned in this book. Especially, since this story describes the life of the person the Author created and declared "very good" (Genesis 1:31 KJV). So of course, He wants to reveal the true pitfalls of the life of humanity, because of a sinful physical birth compared to Spiritual birth upon confession of Christ, inevitably transforming the soul (emotion, will, and mind) of man in the Spirit. No doubt, the acts of the sinful nature are measuring rods frequently used in society, to determine whether an individual's character earns them acceptable kudos to be applauded an honorable person. Given the ungodly behaviors listed in Galatians 5, it clearly defines the moral environmental influence and guidance driving the person, Spirit, or sin.

Growing up I often heard this phrase, "the apple doesn't fall far from the tree," relating negative connotations about family and neighbors, more than relating positive ones to them. This idiom associated similar family relational behaviors. This was due to repeated family cycles of alcohol, drugs addictions, womanizing, those whose parental provider was the state, the criminal minded, illiterate individuals, and distinct vices. These were often the measuring rods of no-good attritions our neighbors deemed that connected us to our family tree.

Despite this perception, God in his infinite wisdom parallels the apple tree as the producer of good fruit although faulty fruit emerges there and eventually falls from the tree. This fruit becomes defective because it is contaminated by bugs and parasites that corrupt it, changing the nature of the apple. Nevertheless, when the fruit falls it remains close because it was produced from the same tree purposed to produce good fruit from the apple tree. I often heard negative accounts of the apple tree analysis growing up and was sadden that those teaching this illustration never acknowledged that the purpose of the tree was to produce favorable good fruit never minimizing the value of this tree. Isaiah records a tree metaphor regarding the emergence of king David from his father's lineage in images of a stump(tree), branch(descendent) and root(people) providentially denoting that a new heir would eventually be born changing the family dynamics constituting the favor of God, (Isaiah 11:1 NIV).

In the spiritual realm God was changing the Mitchell family tree. Grandma Brooksie laid a new foundation of faith, that despite the contaminated apples from our physical family tree, the spiritual bush was sustaining the fruit on the tree that still had value and those that fell have not been forsaken. Therefore, honorable attribution has been assessed to our new faith heritage by our Father God as fruit belonging to Him, "for you are sons of God through Jesus Christ," (Gal 3:26 NIV). Thus, by faith phenomenal features of good fruit has sprung forth from the Mitchell lineage.

The Biographer wants to appeal to the innate desire of the observer, to comparatively sense the cause of the action and power behind these behaviors and desires. Inasmuch as it defines you as a person and is reflective in your lifestyle. The Creator of this book is the Spirit who dwells in us and is with us progressively working to assure us that we are being made into a magnificent book. The Spirit guides the pen of the Writer in our life to make us into a good book. Afterall, the Spirit inspired the greatest book of all, "The Bible" that is greater than accolades of the recipient of the Nobel Peace Prize.

Being a good book, complements the Writer when the characterization bears witness to the Spirit of the Author. The spiritual Editor is glorified when I have joy and peace notwithstanding my failures and faults because I acknowledge them. He patiently uses an eraser and whiteout to blot out my transgressions and sin, reflecting the character and style of the Writer. God purposely employs the highlights of His divine attributes and gifts in us, admired by others that reveal fruit and signs of spiritual maturity, as the evidence that the Spirit is actively working in us. Thus, bearing witness to page and chapter changes that depict the protagonist as an overcomer. Confessing Christ, and realizing that I needed a Savior, the Author permitted the mistakes in my life, so that Christ could come into my heart to perfect His purpose for new chapters and change in my life. Therefore, the pages of purpose begin to unfold and turn.

"And God is able to make all grace abound to you, so that in all things at all times, having all that you need, you will abound in every good work."

—2 Corinthians 9:8 (NIV)

THE PURPOSE

In a nonfiction book the author describes significant personal struggles, issues, pains, troubles, and pertinent things deeming the individual's life a narrative worth transcribing. The plot is written from his point of view because he is conveying a pivotal message ascertained from the life of this person that is viable for human existence, hoping that the reader grasps it. *So, it is with God*, He reveals His plans for our lives in our trials to turn us to Christ to establish us as divine dignitaries existing as righteous rulers on earth. This is vocalized in Genesis 1: 26 AMP, "God said, "Let Us (Father, Son, Holy Spirit) make man in Our image, according to Our likeness [not physical, but a spiritual personality and moral likeness]; and let them have complete authority over the fish of the sea, the birds of the air, the cattle, and over the entire earth, and over everything that creeps *and* crawls on the earth." Then, God set man in the Garden of Eden to work it continuously guided by the presence of God until sin actuating the rebellious nature in humanity entered the garden separating God and man.

Thus, the pivotal word here is "plan." The Greek word for purpose is *boúlomai,* which describes having the determination and intentionally applying wisdom as the impetus to fully accomplish this purpose. The Planner is always faithful to His intent since it is paramount for historical advancement (Biblehub, 2020). Purpose is the will of God for human existence. I know now that all the things I endured, and the ongoing life challenges in my life was the only way the Creator, could impress upon me the need for Christ, whose grace is sufficient for functional existence in this world. I recall, a scene in the movie Coach Carter, when his expectations for his basketball players' academic commitment let him down. Most of his winning team was failing classes. This was a huge disappointment for him, because when the team was formed, an academic commitment was made. Yet, they succumb to the temptations and challenges of life. Because of this, Coach Carter, decided, to put a lock on the gym doors and cancel all basketball games until they fulfilled their commitment to the player contract. When he was challenged by the ignorance of people about this harsh choice, he said," I am doing the only thing I know how to do, to perfect a change in the life of these young men." Upon hearing him say these words, I heard the illuminating voice of God say again, "*so it is with me.*" To perfect a change for the good in your life, I had to permit pain, suffering, challenges, trials, and test in your lives to save you so that you could become the good woman or man I created you to be! God is doing what needs to be done to turn people to Christ because we needed a Savior!

The communal conflicts, family challenges, church hurt, and hostile work environments, not to mention sickness and death were God plots. These things were used as instruments to fulfill His purpose in our lives. Honestly, when experiencing these situations, it is hard to understand that God is working through these circumstances. Sin and suffering draw us to God while the world wants us to believe these disturbs are because there is no God! Evolving from adolescent to adulthood is when the embedded paradigms are actuated in the transformation from a prodigal mind to a purposeful place trusting in God. The lens of your understanding prevails when you begin to glean the glory of your being is only because of the grace of God determining what you were destined to become. "But by the grace of God, I am what I am: and his grace which was bestowed upon me was not found vain; but I labored more abundantly than they all; yet not I, but the grace of God which was with me," (1 Corn. 15:10 NIV). Praise break, praise break!

In retrospect, all the time, I thought I couldn't make it through, and it didn't look like things were changing, I felt trapped, and my situation looked hopeless. Nevertheless, there was a press in me, that never let me give up and as I grew in my understanding about the love of God, it was because of His amazing grace working in my life, family, and circumstances that I am daily becoming what God purposed for me to be, a good book. *So, it is with you!*

We never really consider the impact of our spiritual growth as being demographically framed and applicable to our rearing from adolescent to adult in determining who we become. Demographic is a dual dynamic word derived from the Greek culture meaning people measurement. Demo: audience, reading, hearing what is described as a certain community. Graphic: measurement or objects to sway. In other words, in the communal realm societies have manufactured influences to persuade and shape us into what they want our lives to emulate and promote. Check your external attire, traditions, and attitudes and ask yourself what product you are advertising daily promoting audiences to fix their ears and eyes on you. For instance, Michael Khors, Gucci, Fendi, just to name a few. Do not get me wrong, we like dressing nice, yet worldly attire should never usurp our spiritual attire as faith principles. The Creator of our brand desire and will is that His sartorial is publicized daily. The demographic of every good book is divinely scripted in the narrative. The distorted cultural customs inserted in our lives are the divine measures God uses to keep refurbishing His creation. My reason for clarifying the origin of this word, is that the philosophy of societal trends are cultural influences working to mentally, emotionally, physically, and spiritually manipulate the people God created as His divine brand. Our lives are daily impacted by past cultural dictates and disciplines based on our relatives and relational associations revealing culturalized citizens rather than the Creator's children, due to worldly things that impact our society.

Thus, God contextualizes the narratives of our life stories for the audiences to consider and ponder. God decided to revise, rewrite, and put in right environments what the world had taken out of context. God decided that it was time to give our audiences, something to think about while talking about us. Critics, after perusing the facts about our conditions and the disorderly clan communities will determine for themselves that something happen to change our lifestyles. God decided to transform and shape His brand from earthly to spiritual products for greater advertisements, daily emulating and promoting the Creator's Name and brand. This right here, is worthy to be praised, knowing that the Creator's glory is branded in my story!

I never really had a person I wanted to be like growing up. I did mimic the teachers in school a lot. One of my teachers, Ms. Martin, would always have what I call a snitching conversation with another teacher. They were always gossiping about something or someone, so I would pretend to be Ms. Martin, and snicker like her, because she knew about everything! Growing up, I often practiced being grown. As a child not fully understanding that this label is easily misunderstood. Our family gatherings taught me that being grown was often attributed to the physical model and not the mental perception. Some weekends, my mom would fry fish, fix coleslaw, and sometimes potatoes fries which was the usual Friday meal. Sometimes, she would invite some of my aunts and their children to our house and they would play cards, listen to R&B music, drink, laugh and have a good time. I enjoyed these times, until the arguing and fighting started. Everything was going well, and everyone seemed to be having a good time with each other, until something was said, that hit an unhealed wound in one of them that caused that person to lash out in anger. Thus, literally causing all hell to break loose, disrupting a beautiful family gathering. Being grown did not look too attractive to me then. While contemplating the adult attitudes as a child, I often wondered why Ms. Martin was always talking about folk and why we had so many family feuds?

Ultimately, I learned that these encounters painfully revealed the devasting trio of unmet needs, unresolved issues, and unhealed hurts. The unseen wounds plaguing many families. In hindsight, I realized that my mother and her siblings had been carrying them for years. Because of this, they were influencing and teaching this behavior to us as children, that this is how you handle hurt by inflicting pain on each other. As I recall this, grandma Brooksie taking us to church and our attending Sunday School, was sowing the nurturing seeds and healing bread of God that was manifesting in us as children. I would hear in my spirit at times when these situations occurred, that "the Lord is my

Shepherd, I shall not want, He leads me besides the still waters and restores my soul" (Psalms 23; 1-2). It was like, I was being pushed by the Spirit, to a safe place, when I heard these words. This is a tribute to the Writer who guided the labors of my Grandma Brooksie, who I heard constantly praying "The Lord is my Shepherd," crying out to the only One that could provide healing for our suffering souls. Grandma Brooksie, knew that there was some sick souls suffering in her family. That is why, she pleaded with Jesus for her family, because she knew that we were weak, and needed His strength to be conquerors in our lives.

Therefore, preparations for becoming a good book, were profoundly cultivated in my life experiences and essential biographical tools drafted by the Creator. When I recall mimicking Martin, the snitching know-it all teacher; I was emulating the persona of a person whose character condemned others rather than cultivating good in her peers. In retrospect, my reasons for mimicking her was due to her knowledge of things, and this appealed to my intellect. However, in my spiritual journey of maturity, we must be aware that wrong beliefs, idols, and influences inspiring wrong behaviors. This is what is motivating our children, youth, and young adults right now. That is why, Scripture commands us to "train up a child in the way that they should go, and when they are old they will not depart from it, (Proverbs 22: 6 NIV). IT IS PARAMOUNT. Scripture commands "fathers, mothers, and household leaders, to establish a faith foundation in your home, tell your children about God, from your mouth creating this sacred ground in your homes," (Deu. 6:1-4 NIV). I am glad that Grandma Brooksie took us to church. Seeds were sown there. However, the greatest seeds she sowed in us was hearing her call on the Name of Jesus in prayer, acknowledging God as the Source for every need.

I now understand that I was created to be molded in the image of God and that is who and what my life should emulate. Furthermore, due to my disappointments with the outcome of many kinship functions, which often led to disagreements and disputes, I made a sincere heart vow to seek good relationships with my ancestors. It is not my desire to cause division among us, but to unite our hearts in the bond of love for one another. Especially, when I saw how conflict can divide families for generations due to misunderstandings diminishing the importance of relational bonds. I must admit that, although my family fought when they were with each other; there was an unforeseen power working behind the scenes because their love for each other kept reconciling and reuniting them together. Why, because of the spiritual seed sown in them was auspiciously working from grandma's prayers.

I recall, one Friday night, my mom, and her sisters, Wilma and Juanita were at the table, playing cards, listening to music, drinking, and having a good time. Our married male cousin was visiting with his girlfriend, and she was sitting at the table with them. An unexpected argument broke out between the sisters. But what amazed me about this, was the female guest at the table, felt it was acceptable for her to insult one of the sisters. It was so quiet in the room, that you could hear a pin fall when this woman did this. My mother and her sisters turned and looked at her, and my mother said, "look here "B" you can't talk about her, we can." A few more words were exchanged between them, and this woman quickly left our house. Although the sisters got out of line due to conflict, their love for each other realigned them and they were ready to fight because their sibling was being attacked.

Protecting innocence from what internally was deemed a predator was embedded in our family nature. I recall in my matriculation into adulthood, my firstborn son, was called a "bastard" by my uncle's girlfriend that sent me into a riveting mold of defense, and I must admit revenge. My sister Mae and I plotted to beat her up! When I tell you, I could not rest until I beat that behind. This was driving me because this was an innocent child. Needless to say, it was accomplished. Can you guess where? At grandma Brooksie's house! In retrospect, what was driving me was the internal hurt and memories of what this can do to a child. Recalling the ills of yesterday, all of these were important processional steps guiding and shaping the gifts of God for the ministerial office He was calling me to. Thus, shaping my character and nature to emulate His compassion caring for the needs of people, the Bible deems sheep.

While, reflecting on the essence of the makings of a good book, the Holy Spirit, reminded me "The steps of a good man are ordered by the Lord," (Psalm 37:23 KJV). This implicit directive reveals the active works of God and His determination to sustain us as spiritual soldiers and companions in tune, like soldiers whose steps are synchronized. His divine nature repels our carnal nature and synchronizes the divine spirit of God within us. The essence and image of "good" in us is demonstrated and actuates our spiritual growth revealed in our lives through faith, goodness, love, joy, peace, compassion, temperance, perseverance, and brotherly love showing the character of God in our lives. Therefore, the purpose of God for us all is revealed in conflicts and crisis.

For me, the powerful spiritual seeds instilled in me elevated my faith in God. As I grew the Holy Spirit, revealed the fruits and gifts from the divine vine that God was working in me through trials and tribulations to purposefully transform my image into Jesus the Shepherd, I strive daily to be like. Therefore, my heart will forever, praise His holy and great Name. "The suffering of this present age are not worthy to be compared to the glory that shall be revealed in us," (Rom 8:18 NIV). This versus solidifies that the calamities of life are transforming instruments to perfect change in our lives through the blessing fabrics of grace and faith. Being blessed to be deemed a good book signed and sealed by the hand of God commands praise and glory to the Author of this, my biographical narrative.

"A step in recovering potential is the ability to move beyond your past and to use it to inform and improve your future. We must learn to live with our memories and allow them to be a positive force in our lives." The key to moving beyond all that haunts you from your past is allowing those memories to empower you instead of destroying you."

—Miles Monroe

THE PRAISE

Praise is a doxological credence of words esteeming qualities that honor God as the eternal sovereign source and sustainer of all people uttered in these profound proficiencies in praise and prayer. The Hebrew word, "kabo," resonates with the nature and attributes of God. While the Greek term "doxa" conveys "glory" arising from "dokeō" imputing value determined in the estimation of the celebrant. "Doksa" is a salutary conveyance of blessing to God that justly verbalizes the opinion of what is good and determined as having distinctive worth, (Biblehub, 2021). Doxology is a praise, bearing witness to the acts of the sovereign God in written and public praises. These terms describing praise and glory are important in epitomizing the persona of God for the things He has done, able to do in us, and through us catapulting the perfecting of His Word as the divine human Craftsman. Creation was appraised by God as incredibly good and determined to be useful in the earth to impart kingdom values as dominion authoritarians. God is critiqued and credited as the Self Inspector of what He respected about Himself as good.

The Hebrew word for good is "tobe", meaning delight in a good thing, the best evaluation of one's wellbeing. The Holy Ghost conveyed that when God created humanity, He crafted the best of Himself and saw then even when sin stained it, He had already Self-approved what our destiny was "tobe." His divine workmanship (Eph 2:10 NIV). "God saw that all He made was very good, (Gen 1:31 NIV).

His works were proven in the trials, and tests that transformed our lives translated in the tales of turned pages "as overcomers and conquerors," denoting, "that in all things God works for the good of those who love Him (Rom 8:28 NIV). Not only that, but we have sung the familiar doxology of: "praise God from who all blessings flow, praise Him, all creatures here below, Praise Father Son, and Holy Ghost," in worship services not fully understanding the magnitude and the depths of what God was being praised, honored, and valued for. In essence, God was faithfully working in us to transform His creation into royal vessels that believed by faith we were chosen by God. Therefore, identified as spiritual beings, a holy and royal nation, endowed with priestly persona making us conscious of righteousness relative to our relational lifestyles through the auspices of the Holy Spirit (1 Peter 2:9 NIV). We are creatures that exist as earthy beings but in the spiritual realm walk by faith, adorning radiant robes like kings and queens commanding obeisance from antagonists and reverence from other aristocrats. Human heirs were created as reciprocal reverberating reverence for God, inevitably describing the essence of our spiritual nature as regenerated beings in Christ Jesus.

The plot of the Author in our dramatic quest and conflict was instigated to change the paradigm about ourselves while God was masterfully transforming us into noble vessels to influence change in the life of someone else. When your life is transformed in essence it encourages others to do the same. Therefore, as redefined royal novels when critics talk and peruse your transformed narrative, the Creator ascribes accolades and credit for His production, resources, publication rights and divine references to ensure that there is no plagiarism. Paul describes our life story as an authentic message from Christ that glorifies the owner of every human manuscript, (2 Cor 3:1-18 NIV).

Knowing this, as I near the close of this book, I must praise Jesus for my journey and his marvelous works continuously forming me in being deemed a "good book." Robert Mulholland Jr., in his book *Invitation to a Journey, A Road Map for Spiritual Formation,* describes the hand of God relationally working in our lives demonstrated in the process of us being formed in crisis and conflicts that are unavoidable in life. These methods are the operative means to transform created beings into the likeness of Christ for relational cohesiveness to cultivate harmonious faith societies (MulHolland, 2016, p. 19). Spiritual formation is the process of immersing God's gracious works by restoring depraved humanity through life struggles to fulfill His word that in Christ we are whole, (Col. 2:10 NIV).

This word translates a holistic explosion of profits earthly beings struggle with in comprehending that dominion- minded citizens have grasped as the fullness of God. Being "free and full" in Christ Jesus, released me from an oppressive mind and the suffering of "no." No longer broken, no longer will I allow slanderous names to defame me, and no longer will polluted influences and value vices corrupt the original divine assessment of my good. These were instruments God allowed and used as the destructive contributors that heightened the plot ensuring, what God destined for me, "tobe." Experiences ensuring that praise in this publication manifested in the turned pages heightening the delight of the Author in this Self-Published novel. God is the revealed initiator of our spiritual growth as the book transcriber actively working through the power of the Holy Ghost through the penmanship of grace (MulHolland, 2016, p. 20).

For this reason, I praise my heavenly Father the Lord God and Creator of all people that has been fervently working in my life from cover to close to illustrate that He is the Author and Finisher of my faith that has been pioneering the tales of my life story.

What is intriguing about a good book, is the closing pages the author intensifies to motivate the readers to see their point of view in the story to expound on their written realities. For me, the sentiment and outlook being conveyed in relating myself as a good book is my testimony of faith and factual witness that the Bible is the protype for human life. The book divinely inspired by God, recording the life stories from antiquity of men and women penned by the innate hands of good men.

The Bible contains the sacred progression of the life of humanity. The genesis of this book reveals the divine plan of the Creator, and His will for the dynamics of faith in Christ to secure our eternal heritage and book royalties. Facts forming the foundation of my book, are the prolific three: sin, suffering and sacrifice. These are the reasons that I am saved and praise the Author and Finisher of my faith, enabling me to share the story of the makings of a good book and best seller. This manuscript, although written by my hands is the inspired revelation from the Masterful Creator Himself, using my story to encourage you, to see your life and to view yourself as a good book.

Your life is the story of God's purpose for you. It unfolded in your environment, life experiences, the evil instruments employed to work good in you. It is exposed in the troubling pages as they turn in your life. You becoming a good book begins the day the chapter of your life is emptied of the old you, and the new spiritual creature emerges because of the Christ in you. It is at this time, the turned pages, line quotes, drafts, whiteouts, rewrites, and revision begin to form the manuscript of your life as you are evolving into a good book. Critics reading your life story witness the visible strips of every page and chapter details of the hand of the Writer, in victories and challenges that you overcame and conquered. This section of praise is certainly and rightly due to God, His declaration in the beginning that the human species "very good," certainly, attributes to Him also ensuring that what He valued stayed that way.

However, before I affirm what I ascertain the good of God in my life, this thought came to my mind, "what is considered good?" We know this word is used loosely and attributed to the nouns of life that are not worthy of this esteem. In fact, this term was significant and divinely descriptive in the genesis of life. This was a magnificent "word" establishing the blessings of God in what He created. As a matter of fact, after sin entered due to Adam and Eve's disobedience,God never recanted what He called "very good", although, there was a painful declaration by Him, when the wickedness of men increased in the land, that God lamented, His regret for creating them, (Gen 6:6 NIV). Despite this, God never changed His original statement calling creation "very good." The divine testimony of God authenticated all of us as first-class citizens esteemed by the superior essence of God. We were blessed and called "very good" by Him and our status from the beginning has not changed what He blessed us to be. Therefore, our view of what is considered good quality ultimately has no validity since we are not the final judge of the human heart and character. The dominion of God governs this.

A question was raised by some people regarding Jesus, the self-proclaimed, Good Shepherd, "Can anything good come out of Nazareth?" (John 1:46 ESV). This scripture came to mind, reflecting on the reason praises are paramount in this chapter. This question was asked about Jesus, after calling His disciple Philip. He immediately ran to tell his friend Nathanael about Jesus, praising Jesus, because he believed that He was the Messiah, the Savior, who God had sent to save and deliver His people from societal suffering. After hearing Jesus' name, reflecting on his life story and hometown, Nathanael, asked an honest opinionated question about Jesus, "can anything good come out of Nazareth?" (John 1:43-46 NIV).

I pose this question, to myself, after reflecting on my environment, "can anything good come from Fair Street, aka "the bottom", the Westend neighborhood, and from my family? Can anything good, come from the abuse, afflictions, attacks, heartache, headaches, shame, suffering, the good, the bad and the ugly, I experienced and all the things that I had to endure? Can anything good come from these things? Can anything good come from being called names, belittled, ridiculed, insecure, being fearful, abandoned, brokenhearted, a suffering soul, and the wounds and hurts that had not healed that I carried for years? Can anything good come from my past failures, sins, mistakes, and setbacks? My answer is yes! Not only that, but David also praised God, for his life of trouble declaring that "it was good that he was persecuted, because these things taught him the significance of faith standards and the relational qualities establishing that he was cut from a different fabric, (Psa 119: 71 NIV). So, it was with him and is with me in the prescribed narrative persecution. The preacher in me is ready to run and shout, right now! The little girl, that grew up in "the bottom," life changed when Jesus came into my life. In the words of Patti Labelle, "I got a new heart, that is-attitude."

Attitude is applicable to spirit in the story Moses relates regarding the tale of twelve spies sent to survey the land God promised them. Caleb's mind in this story raises biographic divine reviews regarding his mentality that despite the antagonists in their territory they had the ability to take possession as landowners of their property. Having the right attitude was vital. Ten men succumb to fear and instilled this thought in the minds of others instigating terror in the family. However, Caleb was ready to dominate because he believed he was taking possession of what God said belonged to them. God was pleased with his valiant spirit, originating from the word attitude. One man was picked out and praised by God because he personally "believed" in what God said. Being the one man or woman picked out and esteemed by God because of your personal declaration of faith is truly an amazing and humbling experience. That is why this section praising God is personalized by experience.

My spiritual growth is authenticated by my experience and personal knowledge of God. Yada is the Hebrew word for "to know," which describes what you have learned and recognized about God in your life experiences promoting your personal acquaintance with God. This personal awareness about God is developed and divinely depicted in wandering days that transformed into witnessing declarations as your trust in God was being navigated by situational dilemmas that required faith in the Lord. In other words, situational ironies, that erupt in our environment to define us, and evil influences intended to corrupt what

God has created us to become is impeded when faith in God is birthed. The outcome the world expected is reversed. Therefore, this chapter of praise is personal and validates that I genuinely believed the old things (views, visions, and attitudes) have passed away and that I was released from these things because of my Father's forgiveness. True freedom is forgiveness. This is not a cliché. Forgiveness actuates the loosing of grave clothes that bound the spirit and soul of humanity.

Thus, a new Vickie was birthed in the spirit. Grace began to authenticate me as the new novel, and sanctification began to perfect change in me washing and blotting out the stains from my past, causing me to realize that no longer was I in people bondage nor accepting what folk said about me conforming me to their narrative. Nevertheless, when I was transformed by the renewing of my mind, I realized that there is *power* in believing and living what God said about me: "I am fearfully and wonderfully made, marvelous are they works," (Psalm 139:14). When you believe and live what God declares about you, then you understand you are becoming like the Creator who shaped you into His image and character, restoring you to your rightful status as "very good." In other words, these synonyms commence from "good" describing the nature of God that identifies my relationship with Him: admirable, exceptional, distinguish, great and first-class. Rather than being defined by the antonyms of the world: ordinary, insignificant, common, and second-rate!

When I served in the children's church ministry, this is one declaration I always required the children to quote, with an added decree, "I am fearfully and wonderfully made, *there is no one like me, I make a difference wherever I go.*" This was the Sunday declaration they were encouraged to recite, believe, and live daily. This affirmation was the seed of faith sowing this confidence in them and influential in my development. This verse was decreed and destined to be established as the impetus driving their destiny being confident in their identity. The Word of God was employed and actively working to ensure that their belief in Christ solidified their distinctiveness in Christ to inspire right behavior and character in their lives. Encouraging faith in Christ actuated a greater consciousness in them to exceed mediocre communal identities. Faith seeds were taught and sown to employ the grace of goodness daily in life relations. My quest and passion perpetually are to give the gift of exhortation by always encouraging children, youth, adults, and people that no matter, how people label you and no matter what environment you come from, *it will not change the divine decree of God about you.*

This declaration in essence establishes that God said what He created was "very good," which means men should stand in awe of us. We were created as awesome creatures, distinct and set apart to accomplish things that surpass the earthly environment from which we are birthed. That is why, the psalmist David praised God for this revelation knowing that he was valued before birth, (Psalm 139: 14 NIV). When my own eyes were open to this and I began to believe this about myself, my heart and my life changed because the stains of slander and snags no longer confined and defined me anymore. Slander, insults, and adversarial influences will always exist in this world. However, when you receive and believe the prophetic pronouncement upon your life, and it exuberates new life in you, the Spirit yields a praise to God for coming to your senses regarding your identity. Knowing the truth causes the good in you to arise when you know who you are and the Creator that wonderfully made you!

The late Dr. Myles Monroe was a great leadership orator. He was a renowned spiritual leader whose mission was to cultivate the leader in humanity by encouraging them to change their perception about themselves. His main philosophy was belief reflect behavior. What you believe about yourself is who you become, and it impacts your heart and mind. Attitude ensues from the heart, and he deems this the subconscious influencer that drives your thoughts about you and other people, (Cultivating the Attitudes that Affect Human Action Part 1 Dr. Myles Monroe, 2021). The Bible supports this, "out of the heart comes the issues of life," (Proverbs 4:23KJV). The preceding word of caution in this verse is keep or guard. We are commanded to be watchman over our heart, the seat of our thoughts that dictate our actions and attitude regarding how we relate and respond to the things valued. You must believe that when Christ becomes the Lord of your life, you were the recipient of the fullness of all the riches He embody that resides not in your flesh but faith, (Luke 6:45 NIV). The goodness of God is activated in you.

Now, how about you, ask yourself, this question: "Can anything good come from your family? Can anything good come out of the challenges and conflicts that you have faced in life? Can anything good come out of the things you conquered, and can you honestly say that it all worked together for your good, making you better? If your answer is yes! Then you can admit that the sovereign hand of God was instrumentally working in your life trials and troubles, perpetually turning pages transforming you into a good book and best seller. Scripted by God the Biographical Author and Editor of your faith.

I praise God because every time my life is perused by readers, critics, and the world, I am a visible witness to the goodness and grace of God in my life. Each page of my life and all that I have become, is a testimony to what the Lord has done! If I was you, I would stop, pause, and put a praise ye the Lord bookmark here! God through The Holy Spirit has been fervently working to get good quality out of you being endorsed for final print and advertised by the book counsel in heaven as the next bestseller. Evolving into a bestseller is expressed in our spiritual growth and witness proclaiming the goodness of God, for His Word is true, "we overcome by the blood of Jesus and the word of our testimony" (Rev. 12:11).

For this reason, I share two life changing incidents that capitulated a deeper reservoir of faith emerging within me. The first event was initially omitted and concealed. However, while recalling my life narratives, the Holy Spirit brought this one back since this incident could have potentially averted God's plan for my life, derailed the new chapters and ended my life. My sister, and I were at the laundry mat washing clothes and two guys were making insulting comments and gestures toward us and one of them touched my breast! I immediately reacted to this inappropriate disrespect by slapping his face! He and his friend left, only to come back and he put a gun to my head, and said, "…tch hit me again," and begin slapping me. This dude slapped me so hard, I was seeing stars. While this was happening, I heard myself saying, "the police is on the way, the police is on the way," while he was still slapping my face! (The police had not been called, because we thought they were gone). Suddenly, he seemed afraid and ran out the laundry mat. My sister and I was in shock, after this abusive encounter. My life could have ended due to this horrific abuse that was worse than the domestic grief I had suffered. What resonated with me relative to this incident, is that instead of reacting in fear, faith arose and spoke the deterring words to scare this man away, while he held a gun to my head simultaneously slapping me! After recovering from this encounter, I heard grandma Brooksie prayers, about the Shepherd that is with us in dangers seen and unseen. Surely, I survived this threat because the Shepherd was with me.

Subsequently I later experienced an unexpected health attack diagnosed by doctors as colon cancer a life changing or ending affliction. This affliction arose, five years after being hospitalized for five days for abdominal pain that the test revealed was due to a mass, chromes disease or diverticulitis. After being hospitalized for five days no final determination was made and I was instructed to get a colonoscopy. I did that and was advised to get another one in ten years. Nevertheless, five years later, again, abdominal pain led me to the doctor and this time, test revealed a colon mass the size of a grapefruit that required surgery.

Listening to the doctor explain the surgery procedure regarding removal of the mass. This term was originally communicated to me, even though during the conversation mass was transposed with cancer. During this conversation, the doctor, stated, "Mrs. Warner, what you are getting ready to experience, is going to take great faith." He said, the word that quicken me and there was a presence radiating over me and each time, the "c" word was mentioned, that would not allow me to accept this. My faith had taken a stand and was guarding my heart while the Word of God was initiating providential healing! What was resonating in my mind and heart was to trust in what God said when faced with unfavorable health reports: "I AM the Lord that Healeth thee," (Exodus 15:26 KJV), "Jesus was wounded for our transgressions, bruised for our iniquities and the chastisement of our peace was upon Him, and by His stripes, my body was healed," (Isaiah 53:5 NIV). The

Holy Spirit clearly spoke to me and said, "Be faithful to God because He has been faithful to you." I recall having an overwhelming presence of peace in God's Word because I had faith in what His Word said that He was, and able to do to perfect healing in the body He created regarding this disturbing report.

As a result, of my trusting in His Word, God did what He said, heal me! Because of this, I can praise God for the tests, He deemed necessary to include in this biographical testament to expound upon the good seeds of faith sown in our hearts that grow to galvanize our faith when threatened by unexpected conditions and crises in our lives. The Word of God muscles and moves the mental chains in how these things are perceived routing them out through the vehicle of our faith. Thus, Pistis, is the patented biblical indemnity for faith, that activates divine persuasion to trust in God.

Therefore, faith wins the battle of the mind every time because it is never produced by people but by the proclivity of God (Biblehub, 2021).

The Author and Finisher of our faith employ all rights in navigating our life stories. His ideas are communicated and expressed shaping our purposes through the markers of life and the unexpected circumstances that are highlighted in our faith journey while God is proficiently working on cultivating you into a "good book." When there are no other chapters to add to these manuscripts, and the Writer reviews the final draft, peruses the front and back book covers, stirring contents, images, divine copyrights, this is done to ensure proper credits of praise and glory characterizes God the Biographer. Literary integrity always encourages customary recognition in every novel to "always give credit," for someone else's work or contribution. For this reason, I must give honor to God, for it was His sovereign foundation that orchestrated the early stages of my spiritual growth through the seeds sowed in me by my grandma Brooksie. Seeds that produced a scholar, preacher, teacher, writer, and servant of the Lord. Certainly for this *I must give credit to God.* I am a product of His works and written manuscript. "For we are God's workmanship, created in Christ Jesus to do good works, which God prepared in advance as our way of life. We are God's handiwork, (Ephesians 2:10 NIV).

CONCLUSION

Lastly, well done good and faith servant, is the goal for our lives. Believing that God will affirm His blessings at the close of your chapter should motivate you to remain faithful as the biographical grace of God is actively working in your life. Knowing that you are evolving daily, and God is being exalted in the perfecting of your transformation, while readers are anxiously fixing their attention on the pulsating pages of your novel, certainly reveals the pioneering manifestation of mercy inspiring, and driving your good book conclusion.

Every exciting and dramatic detail of your life draws the curiosity of the reader who inspects your book. Drama and dysfunction motivate barren people because they are driven by the dirt and drama of people. They like diving into the reality airings of other folk lives, as measurement of tolerable trends to distort them in their analyzation as remedies and common solutions for trauma.

Nevertheless, the Producer and Creator of your novel in the pencil and pen curves of your journey, actuated in the rollercoaster of your life ups and downs, inspired a new you. Implemented through the Spirit fervently working purposely turning the pages of your life, providentially propelling every new chapter as your narrative journey progresses the appointed epilogue of your narrative. The Writer hopes to create a thirst in every person reading your life story to encourage and persuade them to seek the spiritual Transcriber that transformed and made you a bestseller.

Moreover, the good that we should strive for in being a bestseller, can only be framed and formed in Christ, who is the spiritual promoter, and divine endorser in heaven, testifying that we have been tried and true, authorizing our acceptance in being called a good book. His endorsement matters. It is His blood that stamped the seal of approval on our autobiographies deeming us first-rate manuscripts.

Not only that, testimony of the witness of Jesus, affirms that our lifestyles depict faith integrity works that are being morally ordered to be deemed a good person, (Psalm 37:23 NIV). Yet, let me encourage you that even in good steps of wisdom, knowledge, understanding, meekness, gentleness, temperance love, and joy that promotes you to strive to live in peace with people, the world will not always respect you. Therefore, do not despair about pleasing them but motivated more in always pleasing God. This decisional attitude impresses that good is greater than grief. Thus, my desire to emulate this light has been the impetus of the good actively working in actions, attitudes, attributing to the honorable attributes for others to deem worthy of esteem, because these are heavenly rewards that glorify God.

The final chapters and contents of our lives are concluded, upon the final review of God, the Heavenly Author, who verbally accredits the finished manuscript in the final analysis and deems and declares that we are to be called an exceptional "good book." In the meantime, earth is encouraging the viewers to dive deep inside to uncover the marks and cross outs in your life, only to discover the essence and magnificent ingredients instilled in you, due to the revisions and revelatory glory of a transformed life because of Jesus Christ. Thus, making you an exceptional book, printed firsthand from glory!

You know why, God was with you and worked all things for your good. Just like God was with Joseph the dreamer whose life story was filled with drama. Nevertheless, in the last chapter of his life the story changed when he gained understanding about all the pain and trials he endured. Joseph's, story changed when he realized he had been healed from all the heartache, in this decree, "it all worked for my good." Joseph made the final print for publishing in the last chapter that he had matured into something good because the Lord was with him." The Lord was with Joseph, just like He has been with me and you. In this last chapter, this too is my testimony, the Lord was and is with me," and all things worked together for my good, (Rom. 8:28 NIV). What the enemy meant to keep my heart tied in hostility, God used as determining factors of purpose and copyrights as the Author and Finisher shaping the destiny of this book, fervently working by faith in my future chapters to translate not just a good testimony but a marvelous story. Not only has God purposed this for me but the divine Novelist has the same biographical plans for you! The parables of this manuscript attributing myself "a good book" are determined by the "why, what and who "providential message in the words of Jesus when he was shown respect for being "a good teacher," then asking the viewer why he esteemed this virtue in him, acknowledging the source that perfects good in human frailties, (Mk 10:18-19 NIV). Thus, Jesus explains the underlying reality of why he perceived this and what the importance of his accolades revealed that is relevant to the Who "good" originates. In other words, good describes the divine nature of God faith ensues characterizing the essence of God in my life, influencing this quality developing me into a good manuscript despite the challenges in my life. For this reason, the Biographer deemed "good" as the title for this book depicting His will for our lives.

While visiting my eldest aunt one day, my mind reflected on my Grandma Brooksie and her impact in my life because of the seeds of faith she sowed in me and my family. She was sitting on the porch, and we were reminiscing about our family sorrows and successes. Then, she showed me her flowerpots, subsequently getting up and going inside the house and came out with a picture of a vegetable plant that had, "porch plants" written on it. My aunt said, "I sit here on the porch every day and drop seeds into my pots and wait for my plants to grow." My spirit jumped. It was at that time, that I heard the Holy Ghost say, "that is what your grandma Brookise did," every weekend when her children and grandchildren showed up at her house, she dropped seeds in each of you. We were the pots. We were empty and worthless pots she would always put soil in to encourage our hearts and minds and then she would drop good seeds in this soil. Seeds, from Sunday School, which is the Word of God and her fervent seeds of prayer! Now, remember, grandma always put us out, after our weekend stay. Why, because some pots with seeds must be put out to grow. This revelatory depiction taught me why she put us out. Grandma Brooksie was waiting for the seeds, she sowed in each of us to take root and grow. I give glory to God because her seeds are still manifesting in my family and growing! Her prayers were heard and are still working by faith cultivating the Mitchell soil. Grandma Brooksie is resting in glory, and I am sure she is pleased that her prayers are laboring, and that her pots are producing because she sowed the seed of faith during her lifetime. Therefore, this book honors her memory and legacy. I am one of the pots that God is manifesting the seeds of my grandma Brooksie in, shaping His divine nature and goodness in my life, daily making me print ready with a glorious ending! Therefore, I encourage you to sow good seeds in the pots in your children, family, homes, business, churches, your societal and significant domains around you. Start dropping seeds NOW to establish a faith foundation in your family legacy!

Every book of the Bible records the story of the life of an individual whose life was faulty but their faith in God cultivated a chapter change. I close with these prolific remarks by Mark Batterson, from his book, *Draw the Circle*, "God wants us to get where God wants us to go more than we want to get where God wants us to go. And He is awfully good at getting us there. All we must do is follow the holy script of God the Artist because your life is His earthly canvas that He is transforming into His image. God is the Writer. You are His book. If people like what they read in your life, they just might want to pick up the Book that inspired your life authenticating your conversion." The book Batterson endorses is the Holy Bible the divinely inspired manuscript of God.

"I thank my God every time I remember you. In all my prayers for all of you, I always pray with joy because of your partnership in the gospel from the first day until now, being confident of this, that he who began a good work in you will carry it on to completion until the day of Christ Jesus.

It is right for me to feel this way about all of you, since I have you in my heart and, whether I am in chains or defending and confirming the gospel, all of you share in God's grace with me. God can testify how I long for all of you with the affection of Christ Jesus.

And this is my prayer: that your love may abound more and more in knowledge and depth of insight, so that you may be able to discern what is best and may be pure and blameless for the day of Christ, filled with the fruit of righteousness that comes through Jesus Christ—to the glory and praise of God."

—Phillipians 1-11

PROPHECTIC POSTSCRIPT

Good extends from God the Father the source of every good and perfect gift. Good is the essence of sight. Good is essential and sacrificed. Good is the evidence of an exit. Good is the emptying of self and the entrance of the sustaining Savior setting and settling God as your divine Source. Good extends from God the Father that actuates a sowing eagle nature that is preordained for you as overcomers and conquers in every storm. Good in your life is purposed for worldwide distinction and revelatory knowledge for all nations to know that God is the Source, the Author and Finisher of your uniqueness and exquisite life story manifesting and matriculating in the tales of your daily existence! Every eye and hand touching this manuscript God has activated an accelerated grace of *good* in your life, effective Now! Revised and preexisting plots are employed to toggle the pages of your life adding check marks of favor in abundance flowing in waves of blessings to beguile your viewers!

THIS BOOK IS IN MEMORY OF GRANDMA BROOKSIE

Honoring a person's memory is the biographical account recalling the deeds, and teachings that elicit a praise for their contributions in changing your life. Because of Grandma Brooksie, I know and have a faith relationship with Jesus Christ, the Lord my Shepherd!

"The LORD is my shepherd;
I have all that I need.
He lets me rest in green meadows;
he leads me beside peaceful streams.
He renews my strength.
He guides me along right paths,
bringing honor to his name.
Even when I walk
through the darkest valley,
I will not be afraid,
for you are close beside me.
Your rod and your staff
protect and comfort me.
You prepare a feast for me
in the presence of my enemies.
You honor me by anointing my head with oil.
My cup overflows with blessings.
Surely your goodness and unfailing love will pursue me
all the days of my life,
and I will live in the house of the LORD
forever".

—Psalm 23

"You are our letter, written in our hearts and known and read by everyone."

—2 Corinthians 3:2 ISV

ABOUT THE AUTHOR

Vickie Warner is an ordained minister, retiree of Fulton County Superior court after faithfully serving there for 22 years. Founder of R.E.S.T. Outreach Ministry. Founder of FLAME, a family-oriented ministry cultivating family relationships. A graduate of Beulah Heights University earning a Bachelor and Master of Arts Degree in Religious Studies. She is the author of Easter Now, a book compiled of Easter speeches and poems that are recital seeds deposits anointed by God ordained to manifest in the life of a child. She is married to retired Sgt. First Class, Avery Warner and together they have five children, Chris, Avery, Brandon, Zenitha and Deontay. Six grandchildren, Deja, Marien (champ), Chris II (Deuce), Aubrey, Christian, Mallory and Dallas. In addition, to a host of family and friends especially dear to her heart.

"But whatever I am now, it is all because God poured out his special favor on me—and not without results. For I have worked harder than any of the other apostles; yet it was not I but God who was working through me by his grace."

—1 Corinthians 15: 18 NLT